D1596478

SPOON

SPOON
DANIEL ROZENSZTROCH

PHOTOGRAPHS FRANCIS AMIAND

PUBLISHER SUZANNE SLESIN

CREATIVE DIRECTOR FREDERICO FARINA

MANAGING EDITOR KELLY KOESTER

POINTED LEAF PRESS

CONTENTS

THE SUBCONCIOUS OF A SPOON COLLECTOR

Should we look behind the extraordinary collection of spoons that Daniel Rozensztroch presents in this book for obscure, deeply hidden reasons that might have motivated him to accumulate, collect, and organize these objects? A relentless traveler, he explored the world, examining and delighting in these modest objects of everyday life and, not satisfied merely with looking at them, he began to construct a meaningful collection that gradually assumed a unique shape of its own.

As he likes to say, a single object does not tell a story, but a group of objects or a collection can create a story. Perhaps these spoons reveal something about the uniqueness of Rozensztroch's own story.

A wholesome and amusing joke comes to mind with an element of truth that relates to the question of what on Earth could possibly be driving him to collect these spoons.

In a close-knit, practically inseparable family in which the children are the apple of their parents' eyes, a young, good-looking boy, apparently intelligent and quick-witted, has been enjoying a normal, happy childhood, except for the fact that he has never spoken a word nor uttered a sound. The parents are completely devastated.

One evening, the family is sitting at the dinner table and the boy suddenly says: "This soup is too salty." Everyone gets up to embrace the child, asking him: "What was wrong all of these years? Why didn't you say anything?"

He replies: "I had nothing to say, because until now, everything was perfect."

The story ends here, raising a host of interesting questions.

In what sort of loving, coddled, sunny environment must our collector have been raised that his entire mental and psychological universe came into being with the touch of a spoon to his lips?

For the newborn, the maternal bond is primary, providing him with a solid foundation and a way of making sense of the world in peace and serenity; the British psychoanalyst Donald Winnicott speaks of the "good enough" mother, who ensures that the child makes a smooth transition from the breast to the spoon without feeling abandoned or rejected.

Could the spoon symbolize an impending separation for the child? Perhaps this newly gained independence, beneficial for both child and mother, marks the beginning of a new relationship between them.

In Ashkenazi Jewish families like Daniel's, who were afflicted by World War II, the fear of going without food and being unable to properly provide for one's children (the constant "Are they getting enough to eat?") presented a daily struggle.

Throughout his travels over the years, Daniel has maintained a fascination with these modest utilitarian objects that are universal in their simplicity across all cultures and which, regardless of material or origin, are used to prepare meals, combine ingredients and, ultimately, to eat. The doting and protective mother is convinced that a well-fed child will always be healthy.

If too much is never enough, will the spoon collector ever stop collecting? Perhaps at a certain point, when he is satisfied.

I wonder if Daniel would be willing to recline on a couch and tell us more about himself, his interest in spoons and his role as a collector.

We decide to meet to explore this question: Is the collector driven by a particular pathology that must be uncovered and analyzed? He foregoes the sofa in favour of an armchair and agrees to shed some light on this facet of his personality.

What follows is something between an interview and an initial session with a prospective therapy patient. I ask myself, "How can we ensure that both collector and therapist leave the meeting satisfied?"

On the one hand, the collector is already well-versed in speaking about his work. He's been interviewed by journalists, television reporters, and a variety of media outlets about his life, his career, and his interests.

On the other, the therapist, accustomed to having conversations with patients that sometimes verge on the intrusively personal, wants to catch his patient off-guard and surprise him.

We decide to give it a try.

He arrives looking sophisticated, his clothes stylish but not showy, a combination of elegance and discretion. He is relaxed and speaks fluently, his words carefully chosen. "Here is a man with a structured mind," I think. This will be a productive conversation.

No, no illness here; he displays no apparent symptoms. "We won't have much to treat," I think to myself, but then, this isn't a therapy session.

I try to put these thoughts aside, but my professional instincts get the better of me.

A sunny, carefree life is unusual, even suspect. To my mind, a person does not become as successful as Daniel, respected for his skills, point of view and expertise, without being driven by a strong will and desire to reveal a part of himself and communicate it to others.

In answering my questions, he opens up and retraces his development from young child to teenager to adult. Opening up isn't easy for him. "I'm a narcissistic person, it's true. I like to reveal parts of myself but I also dislike it, because ultimately it makes me uncomfortable, since I'm never really happy with myself or my image."

Finally, the hint of a symptom?

I ask how he manages this discomfort. "Now I'm more accepting of it, and I've come to own it."

Apparently, over the years, his uncertainty and self-questioning have become overshadowed by work, purposeful activity, and projects that are meaningful to him. In my profession, we call that sublimation.

He describes himself as a methodical, hard-working person who does not like spontaneity and who has become proud of his work over time, despite doubts and occasional uncertainty.

He agrees to take us back in time.

As we know, the foundations of contentment and creativity are established during childhood.

"From a very young age, I was already decorating, using shoeboxes. My parents quickly saw my interest in art and encouraged me to pursue it, which allowed me to thrive."

He says that the overarching theme of his life has been his interest in juxtaposition, alluding to his dual cultural upbringing in which the corned beef & pickle sandwich and the afternoon snack of bread & chocolate coexisted as expressions of a unique cultural history.

For his Ashkenazi Jewish family, the years following the war were a critical period for identity formation: "I'm very attached to my identity, my relationship to my family, and my dual cultural background."

We naturally come to the topic of his interest in objects, especially everyday things with a history and a past, as well as old and rare objects that tell a life's story.

Reflecting on his studies and professional life, he describes his difficulty in adopting a conformist mentality and how he became who he is today.

"Since my studies in interior design, I have always felt torn between the aesthetic imperatives of the time, the things that were presented as the ideal to be emulated, and my true personal tastes. I was a good soldier, but I quickly learned that I could begin to accept being different."

Today, popular art—the large numbers of artisanal objects that Daniel brings back from his trips, and his enduring fascination with handcrafted art is at odds with the spirit of his time.

"My perspective was not accepted, and I felt like an acrobat suspended between the world of design (theoretically, more aesthetically sophisticated) and the world of everyday objects. In the thirty years of my professional life, I've shown what I love and what I've wanted to share. I like to please others and I need their feedback on my work."

I ask our collector, the master of stylistic juxtaposition, how he deals with recognition. "First of all," he says, "you have to earn it, and I'm a very ethical person. I never went after it, I never made a career plan. Reflection is what interests me." He concludes by saying: "I'm not an artist; I make applied art." Now that the internal conflict has momentarily subsided, he is at peace with himself. "It's time to end the session," the therapist thinks, even though there are still lots of questions to be asked. And then the collector starts up again—true to his acquisitive nature, he can't resist...

Normal or pathological, doctor?

—SUZANNE CZERNICHOW PH.D

WOOD

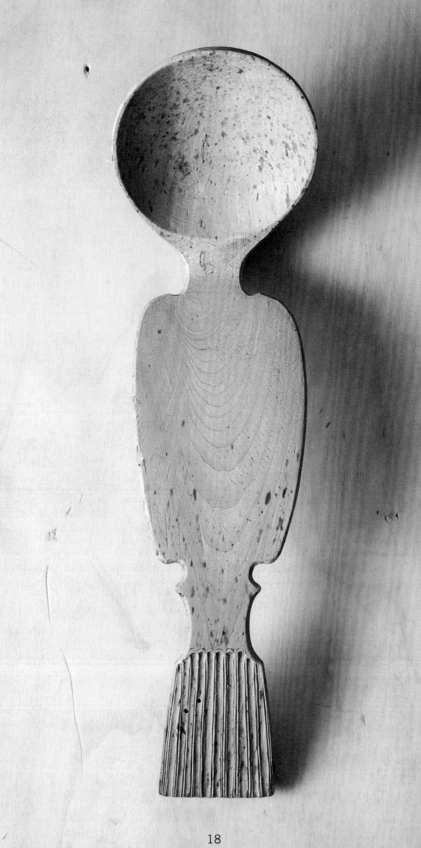

Y F

2891

JAPON

GLASS

44

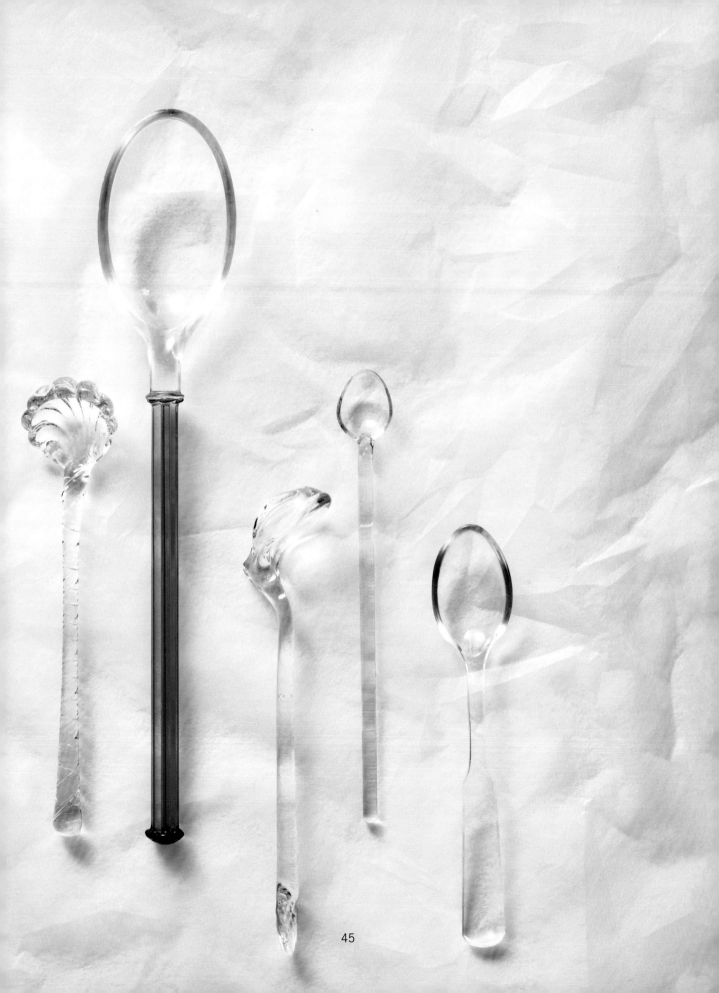

MOTHER
OF
PEARL

54

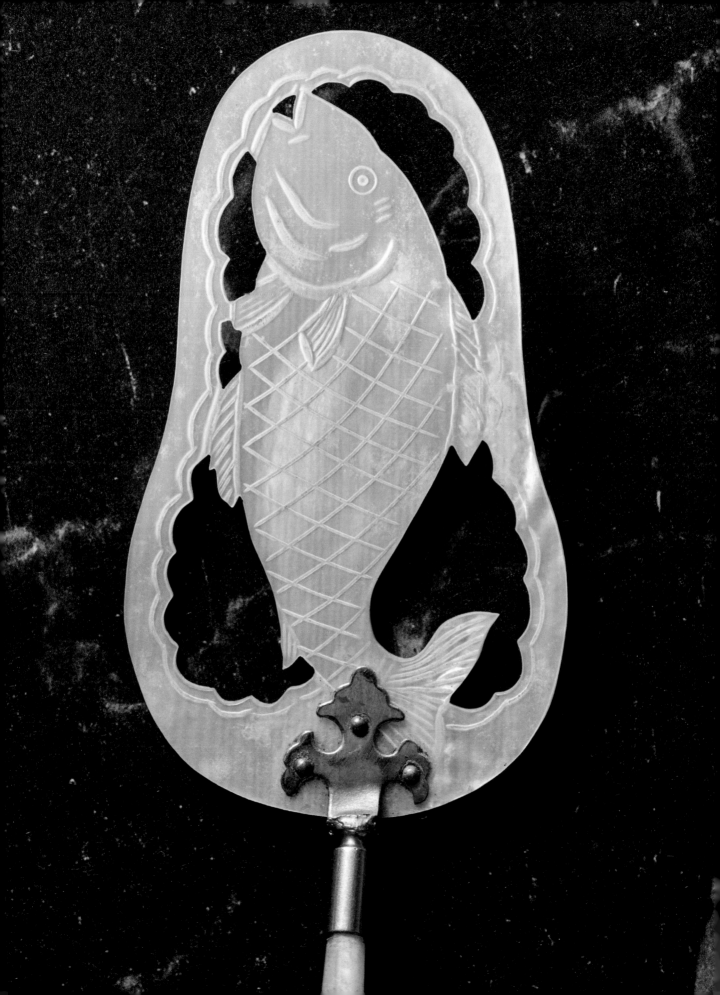

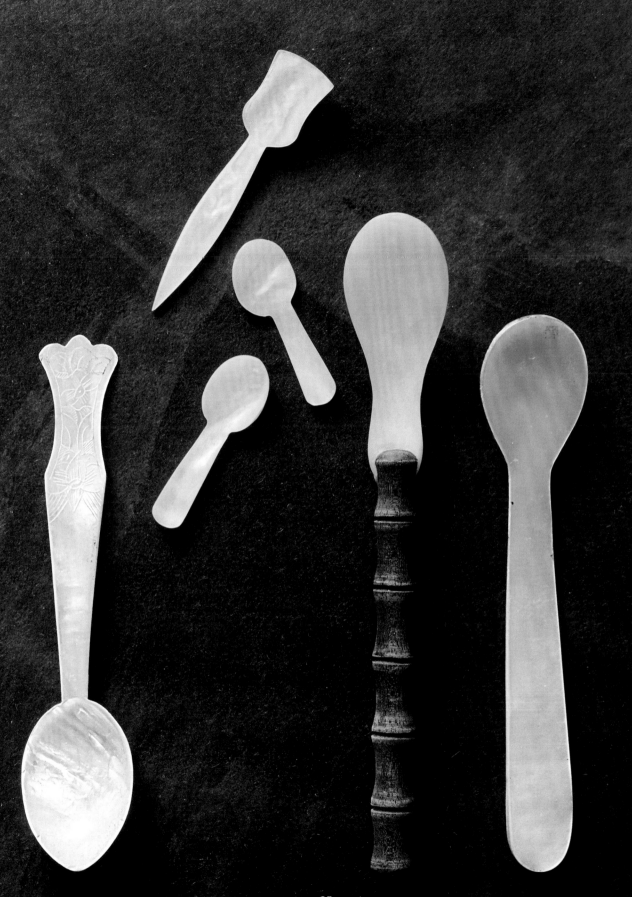

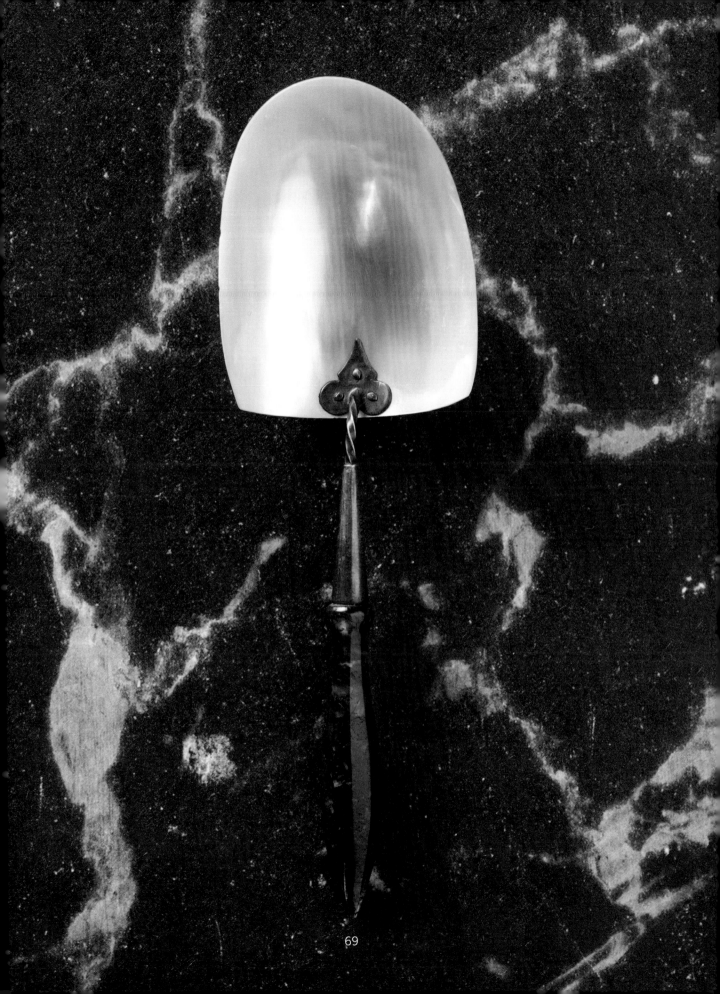

74

BONE

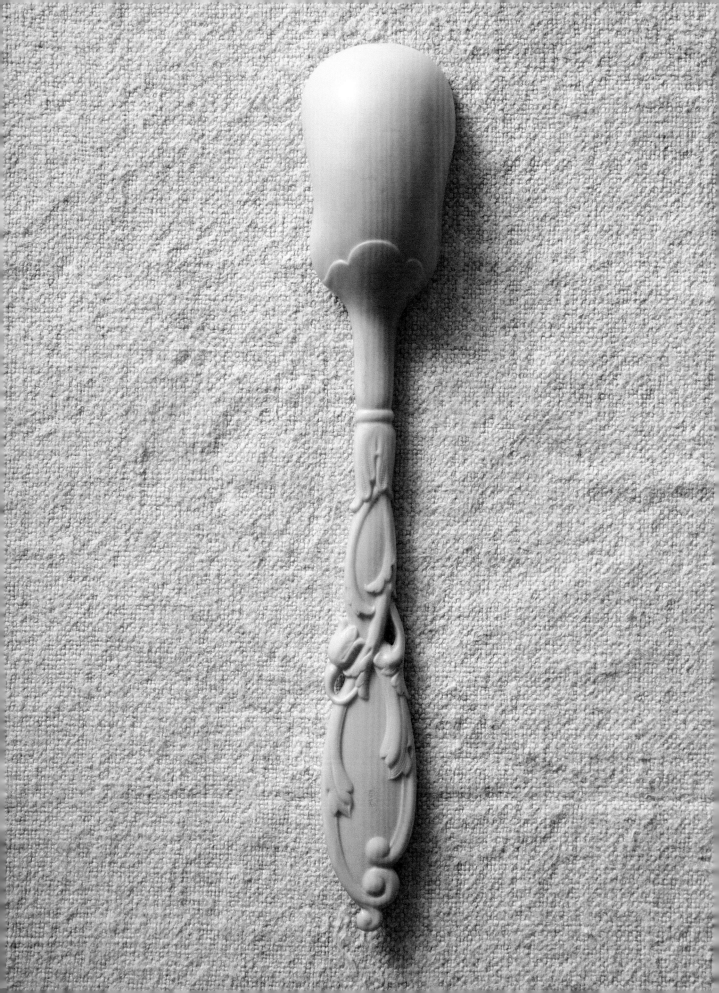

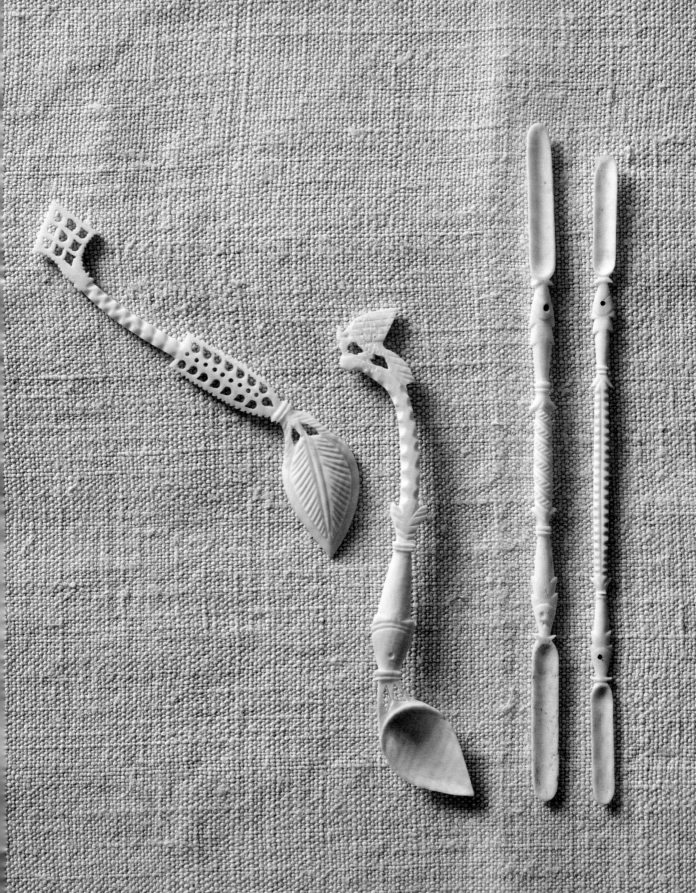

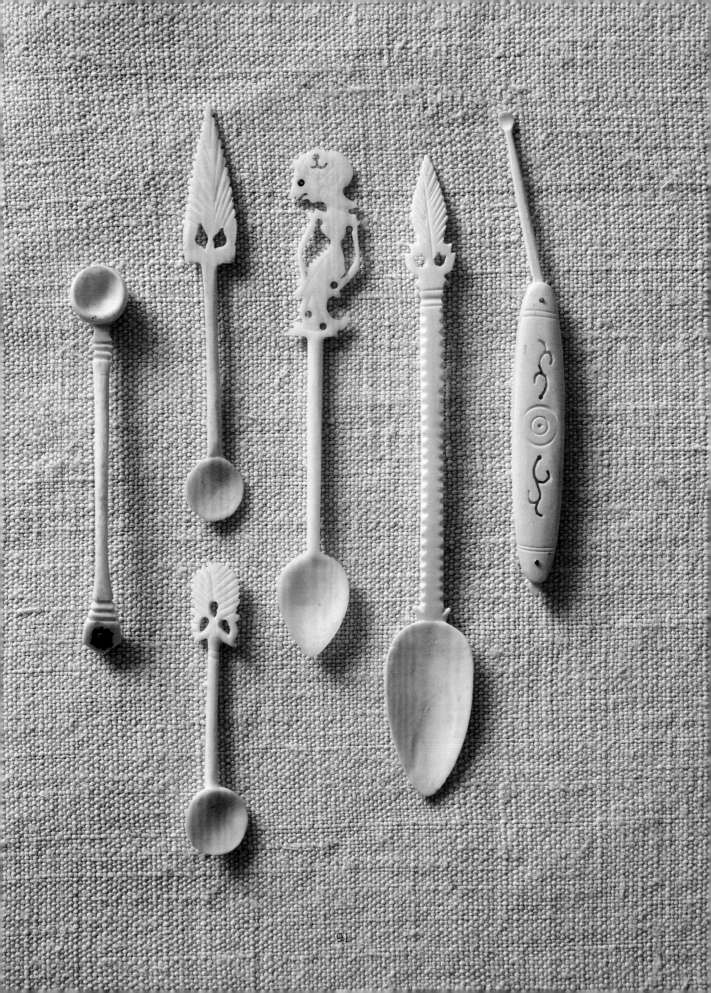

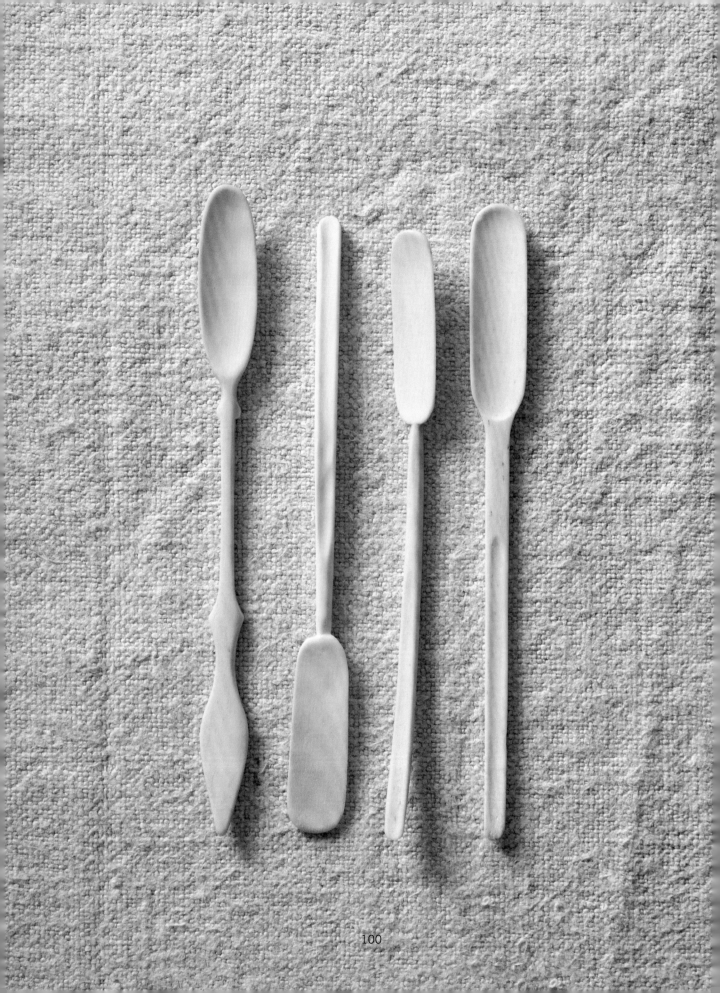

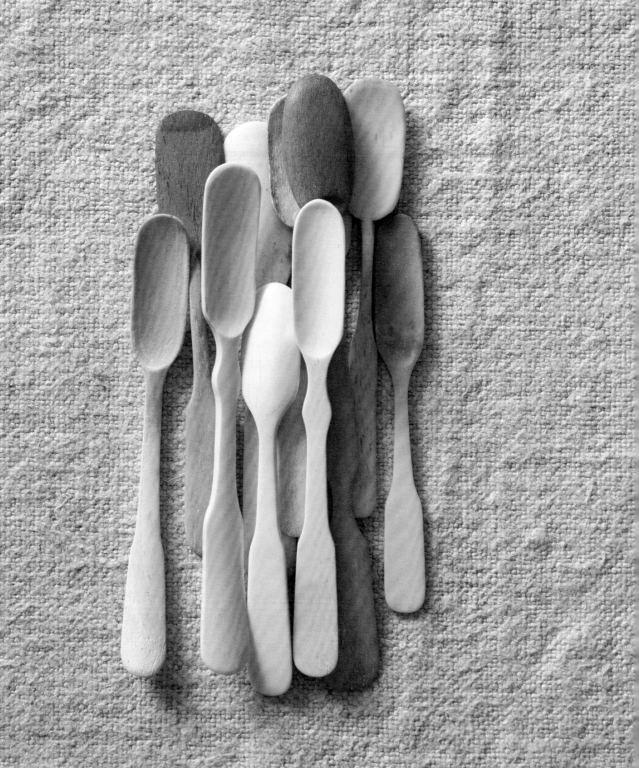

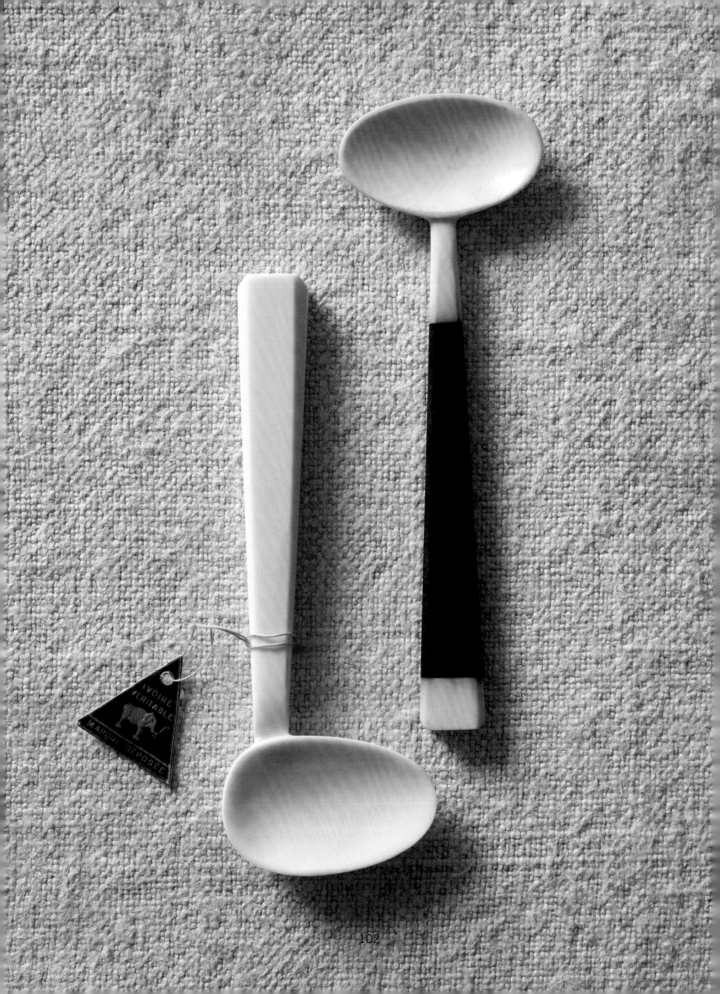

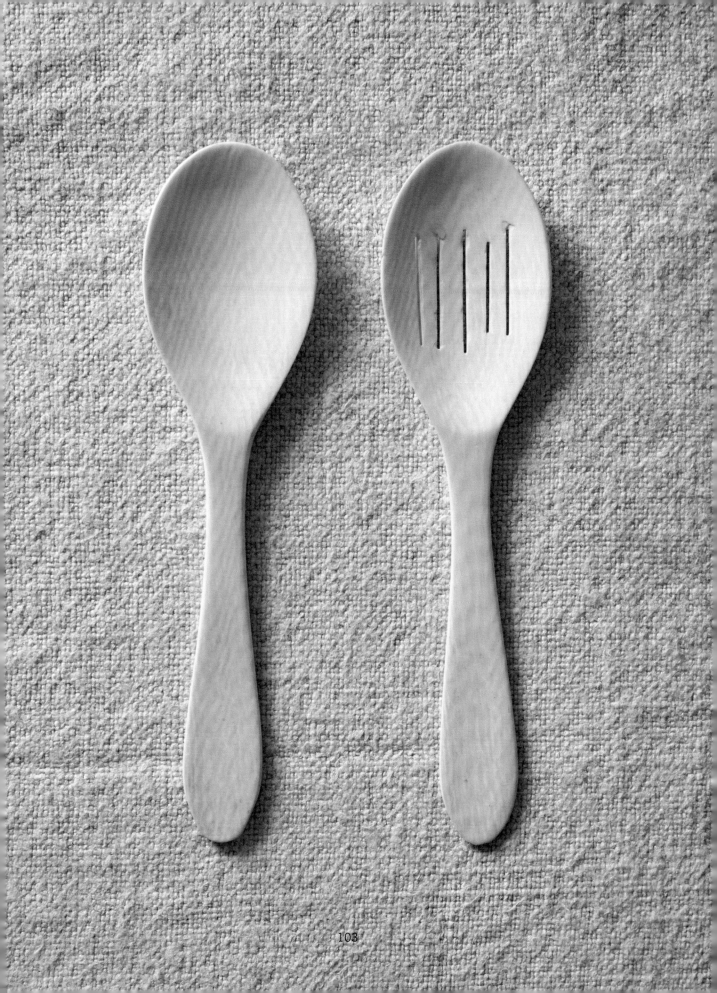

METAL

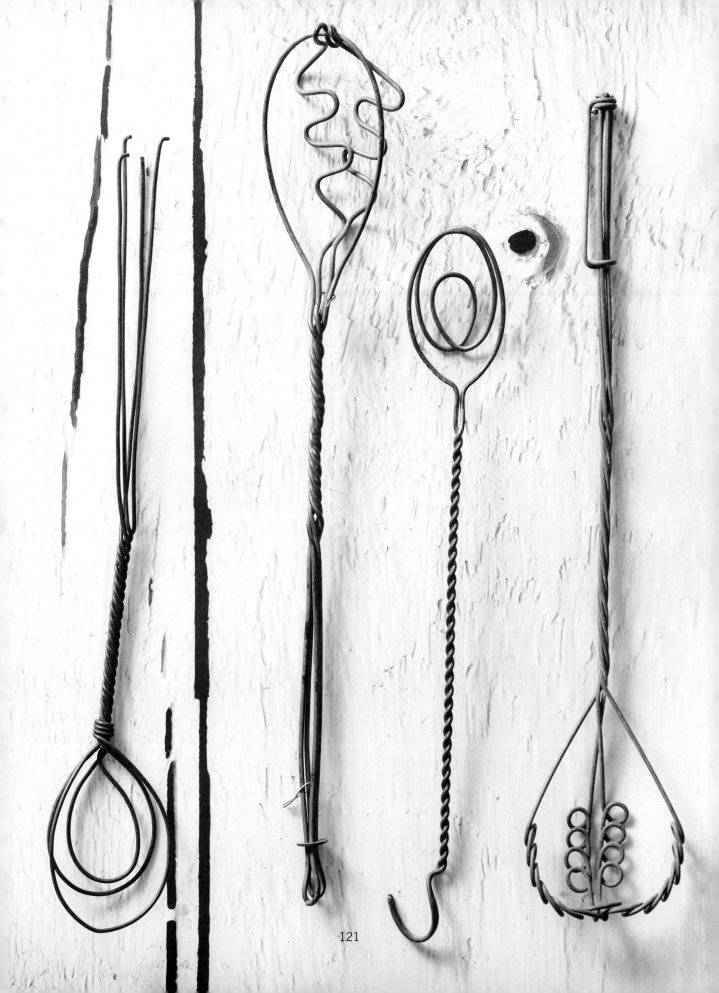

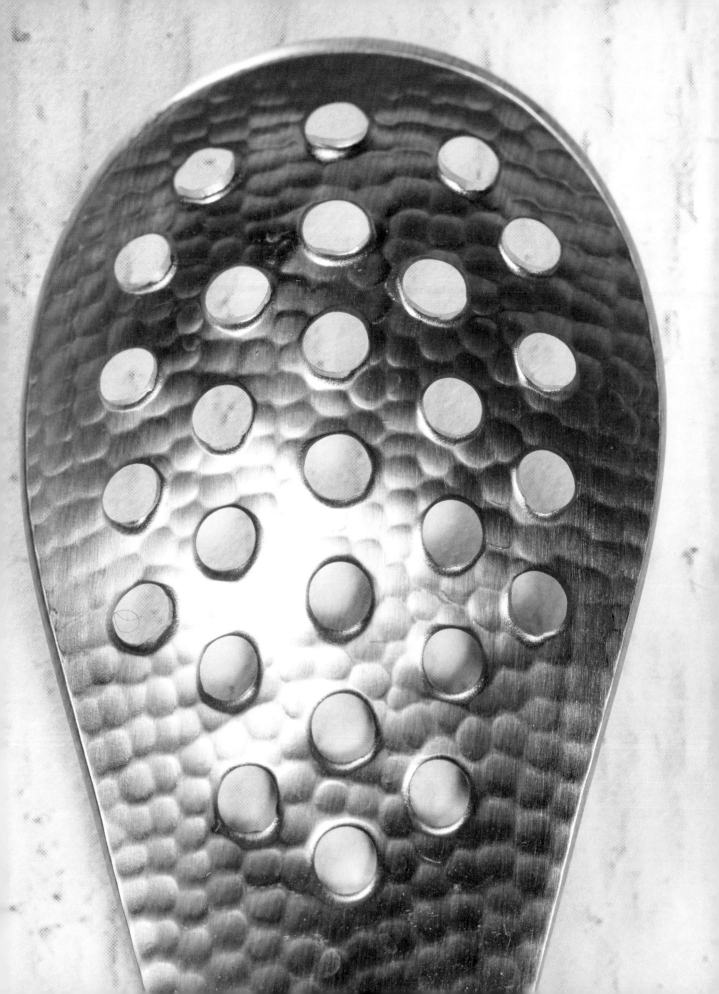

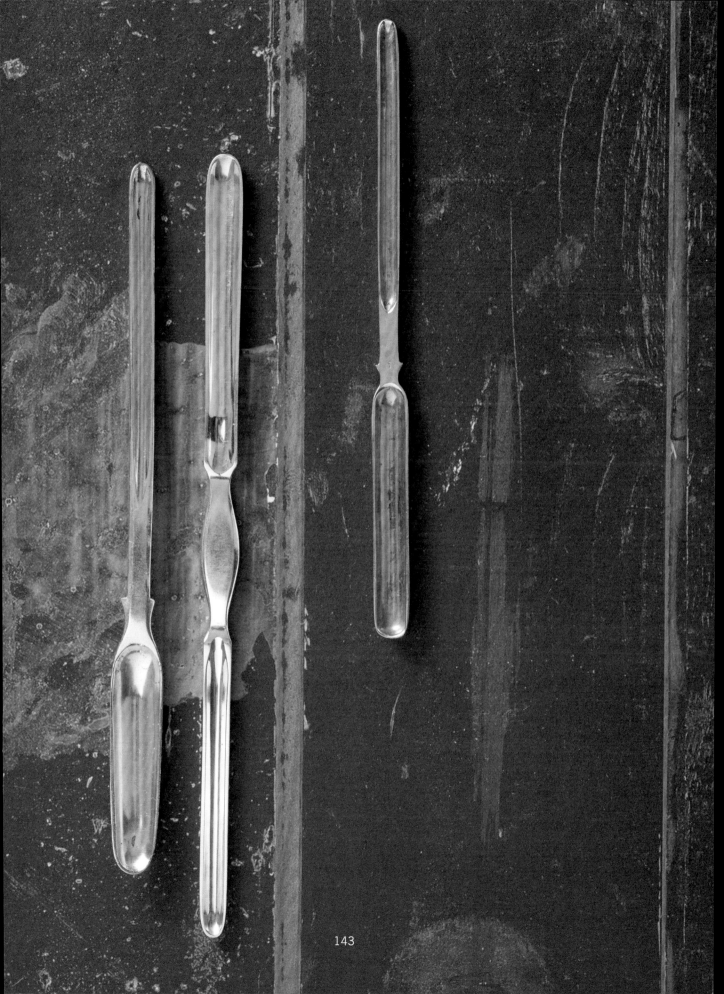

HORN

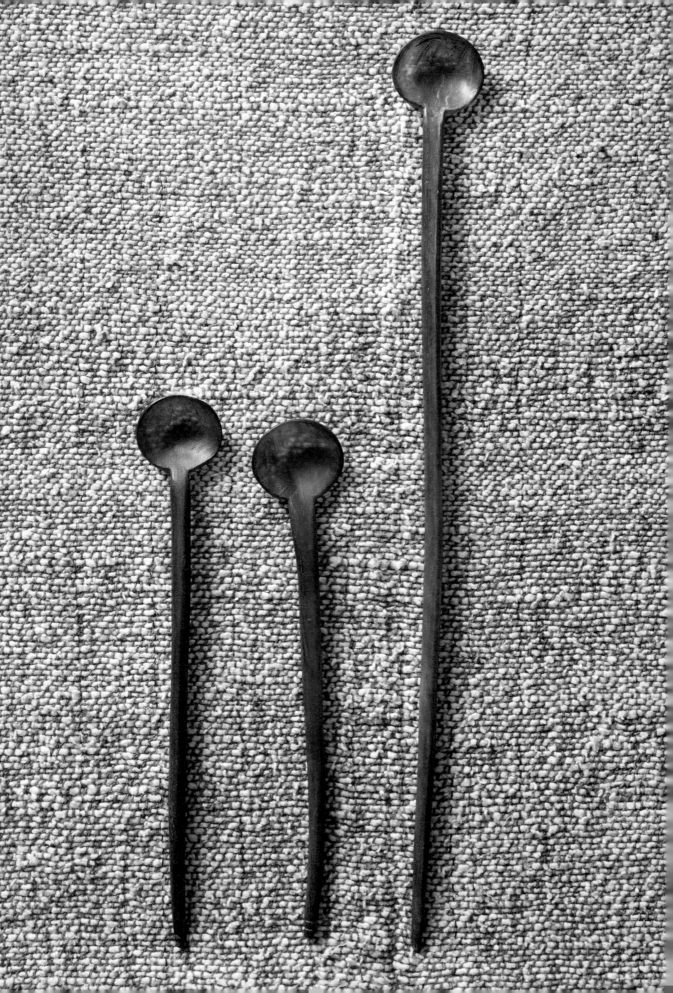

CERAMIC

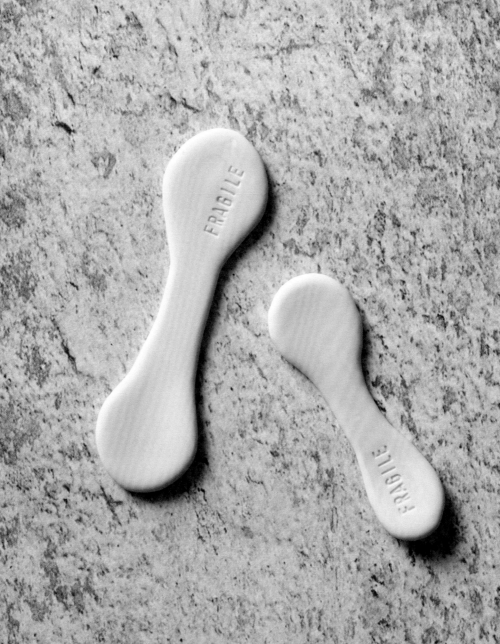

ENAMEL

PORCELAIN

201

A NOTE ON DANIEL ROZENSZTROCH'S COLLECTION OF SPOONS

For years and years, Daniel Rozensztroch traveled the world, stopping in at every flea market or antiques fair he could, looking for the everyday objects of his predilection—hangers, brushes, wire baskets, and much more. Beginning about 13 years ago, another object caught his clever and discerning eye: the spoon—soon becoming one of his favorite and one of the longest-lasting of his obsessions. Through his travels to different countries—from the United States to Africa, Eastern Europe, and Asia—the spoon has been a loyal point of reference, a tactile connection to his many trips. It was the simple spoon that particularly interested him—the ones with an artisanal quality, whether made of plain materials, such as wood or metal, or of more precious ones, such as bone, coral, or ivory. All have a sense of sophistication and originality. Even though some are rare collectors' items, most are as usable today as when they were first made. Rozensztroch's cache numbers over 2,000 spoons, and while most are anonymous, the spoon on the front cover and on pages 8–9 came from Digoin, a long-established French company, while some of the others were created by a roster of international contemporary artists, designers, jewelers, and craftspeople. These include: the baker's dozen, or 13 wooden spoons by Sir/Madam, pages 36–37; the glass implements by Laurence Brabant, pages 39 and 40; the metal ones by Gabi Veit, pages 108–109, Naho Kamado, page 115, Michael Michaud, page 126, and Alexa Lixfeld, page 140; ceramic examples by Patricia Vieljeux, pages 180–181, Clementine Orillac, page 182, Natasha Kaleropoulo, page 183, and Julie Tzanni, page 184; the porcelain ones by Caroline Swift, page 203, and Ted Muehling, the red one, page 204, and the second from the left, page 205.

And it's not over yet. Rozensztroch is still as curious, still on the hunt, and still in awe of the many creators who have taken such a basic item and transformed it into an ultimate object of interest and affection.

TO SONIA, MY LOVING MOTHER, WHO FIRST BROUGHT A SPOON TO MY MOUTH

ACKNOWLEDGMENTS

I first want to thank Suzanne Slesin, my friend, editor, publisher, and the enthusiastic witness of my excesses; Frederico Farina, sensitive artistic director of my obsessions; Francis Amiand, attentive photographer to my needs; Paola Navone, who shares a long-time passion for spoons with me; Rick Vintage who generously offered his entire range of NLXL wallpapers for the styling of our photo shoot; and Suzanne Czernichow, who kindly took on the role of a "confidential therapist" to write the preface to this book.

I also thank everyone who has helped and supported me in the relentless pursuit of this beautiful object: William Aidan, Gladys Amiel, Catherine Ardouin, Laure Amandine Beraud, Marie-France Cohen, Anne Desnos, Françoise Dorget, Genevieve Dortignac, Adrienne Dubessay, Brigitte Durieux, Ako et Shinobu Emoto, Cathie Fidler, Nicolas Flachot, Jérome Galland, Servane Gaxotte, Arthur Gerby, Marion Grau, Thierry Grundman, Corinne Jourdain, Lydia Kamitsis, Laurence Leclerc, Jacques Lefebvre-Linetzky, Valerie Mathieu, Hélène Maury, Jean-Louis et Marie-Jeanne Ménard, Jules Mesny-Deschamps, Christine Puech, Isabelle Reisinger, Catherine et Marcel Sabaton, Mark Eden Schooley, Shiri Slavin, and Claude Vuillermet.

DANIEL ROZENSZTROCH has been a longtime consultant to the magazine *Marie-Claire Maison* and is now the creative director of the Merci shop in Paris, France. He is also the co-author of a series of titles in the Style Series published by Clarkson N. Potter, as well as a number of books on the subject of everyday things that include *Wire* and *Kitchen Ceramics* (both, Abbeville Press); *Glass* (Harry N. Abrams); *Hangers* (Editions Le Passage); *Brush* (Pointed Leaf Press); and *Herring* (Pointed Leaf Press).

SUZANNE CZERNICHOW is a psychiatrist, psychoanalyst, member of the Société Psychanalytique of Paris, family therapist, and member of the Société Française de Thérapie Familiale. She has practiced in Paris for 40 years. Thinking of herself as a true collector, she wanted to face the facts. Three or four pieces and then nothing more! So a meeting with an "obsessive collector" was needed to understand what had happened to make him such an avid collector.

The photographs of the back of the front and the back endpapers are courtesy of NLXL wallpapers.

ISBN: 978-1-938461-42-2 LIBRARY OF CONGRESS CONTROL NUMBER: 2017938951 PRINTED IN ITALY FIRST EDITION 7 6 5 4 3 2 1

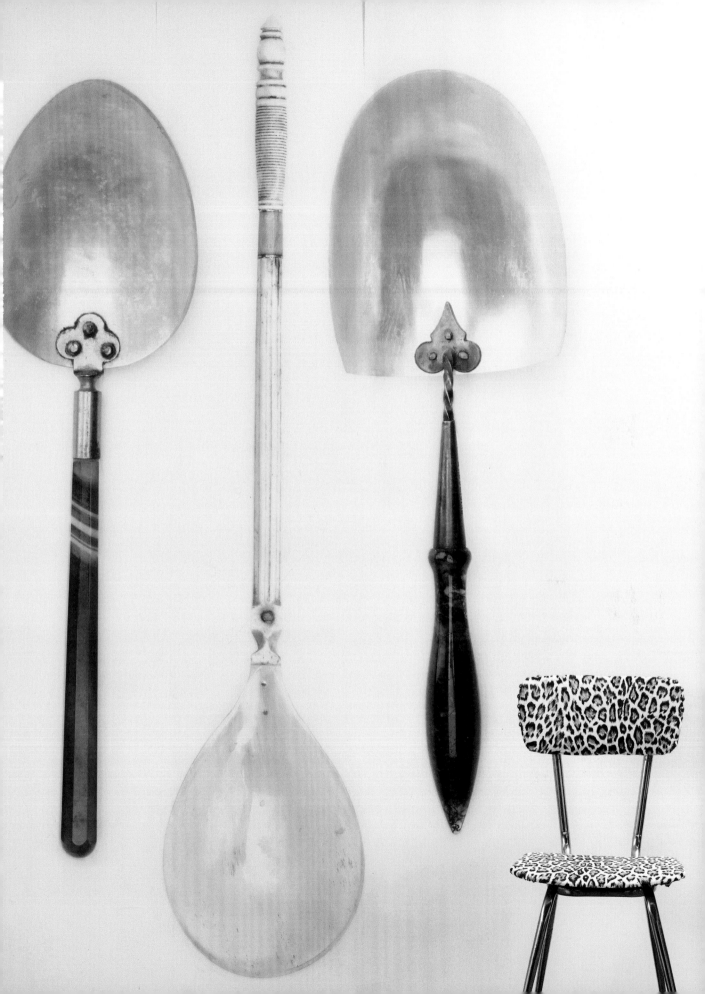